Original title:

Living Untethered

Editor: Jessica Elisabeth Luik

Author: Aurelia Lende

ISBN HARDBACK: 978-9916-86-072-4

ISBN PAPERBACK: 978-9916-86-073-1

Wingspan Unfolded

Upon the breeze, feathers rustled light,
In azure skies, they reclaim their height.
A dance of freedom through clouds so white,
Wings span the heavens, embracing flight.

From cliffs they leap with hearts so bold,
In search of dreams their eyes behold.
To distant lands and stories untold,
They glide where mysteries unfold.

The sunrays kiss their plumage bright,
Guiding them through day and night.
Stars embroidery the velvet night,
Their journey, a celestial right.

In whispers of the winds they trust,
Their spirits soar, wanderlust.
No chains can bind, no iron shall rust,
For in the skies, soar they must.

Among the clouds their tales are scribed,
Of lands unknown, untouched, unbribed.
Eternal freedom, in flight inscribed,
Hearts intertwined with worlds described.

Boundless Blossoms

In fields where petals softly play,
The morning whispers of a new day.
Colors burst in grand display,
Boundless blossoms on nature's array.

Butterflies dance in floral light,
Drinking nectar with pure delight.
A symphony to the senses' invite,
In gardens filled with hues so bright.

Through verdant lanes the blossoms spread,
Like dreams where hopes and wishes tread.
Each bloom a story softly said,
In sunlit paths where hearts are led.

Spring's embrace with gentle hand,
Turns the earth to fairyland.
Each petal falls like golden sand,
A timeless beauty, forever grand.

Boundless blossoms, hearts entwine,
With every bloom, a love divine.
Their fragrance whispers, 'You are mine,'
In fields where endless wonders shine.

Untamed Essence

In the whisper of the wild breeze
Flames of the sun, caressing trees
Mysteries dance in silent tunes
Beneath the gaze of silver moons

Waves of passion, currents strong
In untamed heart where dreams belong
Echoes of adventures call
In nature's hymn, we lose control

Serene valleys, rugged peaks
Wisdom's voice, each mountain speaks
Courage finds its rightful place
In untamed essence, life's embrace

Hearts in Open Fields

Sunlit meadows, hearts unfold
In the warmth of stories told
Fields of gold where we may roam
Love-fueled whispers feel like home

Dawns awake to soft embrace
Dreams align in open space
Hand in hand, with laughter's cheer
In open fields, we lose our fear

Stars align in skies so vast
Paths of love that everlast
In open fields where hearts abide
We find our peace, side by side

Transcendent Wanderer

In twilight's glow, a path unknown
Footsteps trace where stars have shone
Melodies of planets near
Guide the heart that knows no fear

Boundless skies of endless blue
A wanderer's soul seeks the true
Through cosmic whispers, secrets tell
The journey of the soul, a spell

Nebulae in colors bright
Illuminate the endless night
In spaces vast, the soul perceives
Transcendence found in what it believes

Midnight in the Open Air

Beneath the stars so rare,
Whispering winds give chase,
Softly they move with care,
Embracing the night's grace.

Moonlit shadows dance free,
Across the meadow wide,
Echoes of ancient glee,
In silence they confide.

Trees sway with gentle might,
Nature's lullaby sings,
On this serene, cool night,
As time unfolds its wings.

Celestial Vagabond

A wanderer takes to flight,
Among the distant stars,
In the realm of endless night,
Destined for bizarre.

Constellations guide his way,
Through the cosmic stream,
Every twinkle seems to say,
He lives within a dream.

Galaxies pass like whispers,
In the vast cosmic sea,
An eternal drifter's lispers,
In infinite decree.

Break Free the Night Sky

Among the secrets high,
Stars scatter sparks of light,
Dreams take wings and fly,
To shatter the dark's might.

Planets in silent rings,
Dance in orbits grand,
Freedom in silence sings,
As night meets day's hand.

Galactic veils do part,
Unveiling truths untold,
In cosmic art's own heart,
Where night is free and bold.

The Unconfined Pulse

A rhythm beats within,
Unseen yet ever strong,
Living where stars begin,
And where shadows throng.

Its pulse knows no bounds,
In cosmic harmony,
Among the worlds it sounds,
A timeless symphony.

Unconfined, it persists,
In both void and light,
Through endless space it twists,
In eternal night.

Unchained Soul

In the depths of night so cold,
Silent whispers weave through trees.
A spirit's tale, brave and bold,
Breaks the lock, unfurls with ease.

Shadows dance in whispered plight,
Stars ignite the boundless sky.
Freedom found in darkest night,
Unchained soul begins to fly.

Echoes of the past grow faint,
Future calls with siren's song.
Heart and mind begin to paint,
Worlds where they have long belonged.

Wings of Whimsy

Clouds are stitched with silver seams,
Sunlight pierces, bright and true.
Carried high on fleeting dreams,
Wings of whimsy take their cue.

Laughter echoes in the breeze,
Feathers glisten, light as air.
Boundless skies and endless seas,
Whimsical beyond compare.

Magic lies in every flight,
Every turn, a tale unfolds.
Soaring through both day and night,
In your heart, the spirit holds.

Dancing with the Wind

Leaves and petals swirl around,
In a ballet, nature's grace.
Every step, a timeless sound,
Dancing with the wind's embrace.

Waves cascade on distant shores,
Echoes of the ancient song.
Nature's breath forever pours,
Guiding us where we belong.

Mountains whisper tales untold,
Valleys hum a soothing tune.
In each breeze, a love unfolds,
Beneath the sun, and by the moon.

Unfettered Dreams

In the quiet of the night,
Dreams take flight on gentle wings.
Unfettered by the world's plight,
They imagine wondrous things.

Stars like beacons lead the way,
Through a realm where thoughts can roam.
Bounds of reason left in day,
In our minds, we find our home.

Softly, night begins to fade,
Yet these dreams, forever bold.
In our hearts, they will cascade,
Stories of the wondrous told.

Boundless Reflections

In the mirror of the stream
Visions dance, thoughts redeem
Ripples casting silent dreams
Boundless, endless, or so it seems

Skies alight with evening's hue
Whispers weave through twilight's queue
Stars emerge, a cosmic crew
Echoes of the day's adieu

Moonlight graces shadowed trees
Songs arise on whispered breeze
Nature's boundless symphony
Love's reflections, pure and free

Mountains stand in silent guard
Worlds apart, yet never barred
Every leaf with wisdom charred
Boundless tales in nature's yard

Transcendent Paths

On a trail where time stands still
Silent footfalls, echoes fill
Every step a whispered thrill
Transcendence found by force of will

Forests deep in shadows hide
Ancient paths where spirits glide
Mystic realms on either side
Journeys where the soul's untied

Morning dew on leaves unfurl
Magic moments on the twirl
As we dance, our lives a whirl
Transcendent paths, another world

Whispered winds through canyons call
Bringing peace, a tranquil thrall
Finding truth as shadows fall
Paths that lead beyond the wall

Celestial Journeys

Stars arise, the night unfolds
Stories told through lights so bold
Cosmic dance in skies foretold
Celestial tales from days of old

Planets whirl in endless flight
Mysteries within the night
Voyages of silent might
Celestial journeys, purest light

Galaxies in radiant span
Boundless realms beyond our hand
Explorations that can
grand, Celestial dreams that shape the land

Constellations blaze and burn
Guiding lights for those who yearn
In their glow, all truths discern
Journeys where the stars return

Whispers of the Unbound

Echoes in the twilight air
Whispers weave, a tale so rare
Unbound spirits, free of care
Dancing through the night so fair

Wandering past the edge of dawn
Through the veil that time has drawn
In those whispers, dreams are spawned
Unbound souls forever gone

Shadows blend with moon's bright face
Whispered winds, a soft embrace
Every star, a silent chase
Unbound whispers, endless grace

In the stillness, voices call
Across valleys, over all
Unbounded by the earthly thrall
Whispers rise, and shadows fall

Floating Through Eternity

In the silence of the night
Stars whisper tales untold
Time's river flows, so quiet
Through dreams, our souls unfold

Eternal winds do carry
Our hopes beyond the dawn
In shadows we find solace
When all of life is gone

The universe, a canvas
Where thoughts and fears entwine
In endless constellations
We strive for the divine

As galaxies spiral onward
In cosmic dance, we play
Our spirits, ever wandering
In vastness, faraway

Through stardust paths we travel
In search of destiny
Embracing every moment
We float through eternity

Horizons Unfixed

Beyond the hills we wander
Where skies ignite in flame
In endless quest for wonder
Through worlds without a name

Uncharted seas of vision
Where endless dreams arise
We sail without derision
Beneath cerulean skies

In lands untouched by sorrow
Our spirits find their hue
As dawns embrace tomorrows
Where possibilities are new

The endless roads before us
Where destinies await
With courage we'll explore them
Unfettered by our fate

In horizons unfixed and free
Our hearts and minds expand
Finding truths yet to be
In this unbounded land

The Lightness of Being Free

With every breath, we cherish
The freedom life bestows
In moments bright and fleeting
We savor as it flows

Unburdened by the shadows
We dance beneath the rays
In the lightness of our being
We find our soulful praise

Among the whispers of the wind
Our dreams take boundless flight
In fields of endless blossoms
We embrace the pure delight

The pathways we unravel
Not tethered to the past
In the lightness of our spirit
We find our joy at last

As stars align our journey
And heavens bridge the sea
We live in every heartbeat
In the lightness of being free

Blossoms in the Breeze

In the meadow by the brook
Blossoms sway and sway
Their colors paint the canvas
Of this bright spring day

The petals, soft as whispers
Dance upon the breeze
With every tender flutter
Their beauty aims to please

Seasons drift like echoes
In nature's gentle hand
The flowers tell their stories
To all who understand

In the warmth of golden sun
In fields so vast and wide
Blossoms bloom in splendor
Their grace none can deride

As twilight gently beckons
And stars begin to tease
We hold dear to the memory
Of blossoms in the breeze

Starborn Wanderer

From cosmic dust, a spark was formed,
In endless nights, her spirit warmed.
Across the realms, she sails anew,
A dreamer with the stars in view.

Through nebulas and silent skies,
She seeks the truth, no guise, no lies.
With every step, she learns to glow,
A wanderer, forever so.

Galaxies whisper secrets old,
In starlit scenes, her tale is told.
Bound not by earth, by time or space,
But by the endless, boundless grace.

Gleam in Open Waters

In misty mornings, oceans breathe,
A gleam of dawn, the waves bequeath.
The water's dance, a symphony,
A boundless, flowing eulogy.

With sunlit waves, the skies conspire,
To set the seas with light afire.
A melody on breezes cast,
Echoes of the future, past.

Dolphins play in crests of gold,
In open waters, tales unfold.
A world beneath, forever clear,
Awaits the brave, the voyager.

Serenade to the Unchained

When chains that bind are cast away,
A heart takes flight and night turns day.
Each note of joy, a freedom's song,
A serenade to hearts so strong.

Unfettered dreams begin to soar,
To lands where hope is never poor.
With every beat, the truth revealed,
In unchained spirits, deeply healed.

The skies they touch with wings anew,
A life unbound, a clearer view.
A symphony of life's decree,
A serenade of being free.

Odyssey of the Free Mind

A thinker steps beyond the line,
Where dreams and wisdom intertwine.
In realms of thought, he ventures far,
Guided by an inward star.

Each question lights a new pathway,
In search of truths where doubts sway.
On currents of a boundless stream,
He crafts his life, a waking dream.

With open eyes, he seizes time,
The essence of the world's rhyme.
An odyssey of flights untamed,
By thoughts of gold, his mind is framed.

Limitless Skies

Above the clouds, dreams take flight,
Majestic realms in the azure light.
Horizons endless, boundless and blue,
Infinite wonders in every hue.

Whispering winds, tales untold,
Mysteries woven in silver and gold.
Stars align, paths unknown,
Limitless skies where visions are sown.

Nights embrace with a gentle kiss,
Celestial dance in the cosmic abyss.
Moonlight guides with a serene gleam,
Boundless night, endless dream.

Mornings burst with a golden ray,
Promising anew the dawn of day.
Birds sing in a symphonic spree,
In limitless skies, forever free.

Unbridled Heartbeats

Pulses sync with the earth's deep drum,
Love's vast rhythm, a saccharine hum.
Hearts unbridled, wild and free,
Beating in time with the ancient sea.

Passions flare like a shooting star,
Guiding souls both near and far.
Eyes sparkling, love's true light,
In every heartbeat, pure delight.

Whispers soft as autumn leaves,
Embrace the wind, and gently weave.
Stories etched in time's embrace,
Unbridled heartbeats, a tender trace.

Through storms and calm, love remains,
A timeless dance through joys and pains.
In every rise and every fall,
Unbridled heartbeats unite us all.

Soaring Beyond Limits

Rise above, into newfound heights,
Boundaries dissolve in the endless flights.
Wings of courage, strong and bold,
Soaring tales of dreams untold.

Horizons meet with destiny,
We chart our course through infinity.
Challenges faced, fears cast aside,
Soaring beyond limits far and wide.

Amidst the clouds, we find our place,
Glistening trails in the sky we trace.
Stars our guide in the night so clear,
Boundless potential, forever near.

With each breath, a new horizon,
Unseen lands arise, enticing.
Hearts alight with the fires within,
Soaring beyond limits, we begin.

Echoes of Liberation

Chains are broken, souls set free,
In the chorus of liberty.
Boundaries shattered, walls come down,
The echoes of liberation resound.

Voices united in a call,
For justice true, equality for all.
Hearts awakened to a brighter day,
In echoes loud, we find our way.

Steps unbound, paths once barred,
Now open wide, the future starred.
Light of freedom in every glance,
Echoes of liberation in every stance.

Winds of change in the whispers soft,
Lift us high, our spirits aloft.
Dreams awakened, take their flight,
Echoes of liberation in the light.

Footprints in the Ether

In shadows cast by starlit hues,
We weave our dreams in twilight clues,
Unseen, yet felt in cosmic spheres,
Footprints drift through endless years.

Ethereal whispers, soft and rare,
Guide us through the void we share,
A dance of souls in silent flight,
Traces left in the velvet night.

Galaxies spin in silent prose,
History in a celestial pose,
Among the stars our paths align,
Transcendent steps in the divine.

We journey forth on wings unseen,
Through realms that only spirits glean,
A legacy in ether found,
In infinite pathways unbound.

The Art of Letting Go

In the quiet of the breaking dawn,
Memories rise, yet soon are gone,
A gentle touch, a fleeting kiss,
The art of letting go is this.

To hold the past yet walk away,
To learn to live another day,
With tender heart, release the chain,
And let the wounds start to wane.

We find the strength to gently part,
With whispered words that heal the heart,
Transforming loss to space anew,
For growth, for love, that's pure and true.

A journey set by fate's design,
In letting go, ourselves we find,
The endless sky, the open sea,
In every loss, comes liberty.

Breaking the Mold

In shadows deep where molds do grow,
A spark ignites, begins to flow,
A heart untamed, a mind set free,
Breaking the mold of destiny.

With every breath, we suffocate
The expectations others create,
To stand alone, to forge our way,
And carve a path through break of day.

Unshackled from the past's embrace,
We find the strength, the will, the grace,
To shatter chains and barriers tall,
And rise above, to heed the call.

In every tear, in every scar,
We find the light, become the star,
Unyielding, bold, our story told,
Revolution's hue in breaking the mold.

Windswept Bliss

Upon the hill where grasses sway,
In windswept bliss, we find our way,
With every gust, our spirits soar,
A symphony on nature's floor.

The skies above, a canvas vast,
Where dreams unfurl, unmoor the past,
In whispers soft, the breeze does sing,
Of love and life and everything.

We chase the clouds, both free and wild,
With hearts as light as summer's child,
In moments caught between each breath,
A timeless dance, life conquers death.

In every gust, a story told,
Of ancient times and futures bold,
A windswept bliss, forever free,
In nature's arms, our eternity.

Echoes Beyond Borders

In lands where shadows softly tread,
Where history's whispers softly spread,
The echoes dance beyond the line,
A border's tale, a thread's design.

Mountains breathe a silent hymn,
Oceans hum their twilight hymn,
Beneath the stars, where dreams reside,
Echoes float on the night's tide.

Journeys carved in ancient stone,
Every path and tear they've known,
Cross the fields where borders blend,
In the dance that knows no end.

Laughters of a distant town,
Sorrows where the sun goes down,
Each a part of borders' play,
Eternal night, eternal day.

In every step, in every sigh,
Every whisper that will never die,
Echoes beyond borders call,
One world beneath, one sky for all.

Spirits in Liberation

The chains of past, they shatter now,
In fields where freedom takes a bow,
Where spirits rise in joyous flight,
And day dances with the night.

From the depths of ancient woes,
The light of courage freely flows,
In hearts that beat, in lives once chained,
A song of freedom, unrestrained.

Across the skies, a phoenix soared,
In ashes past, new lives implored,
Rising from the dust and flame,
Embracing now, with no more shame.

Through tears which watered seeds of change,
New hopes in boundless fields arrange,
Each soul a beacon, brightly casts,
A glow of liberation past.

Spirits lift in untamed grace,
To find their truth in sacred space,
Bound no more by sorrow's fire,
In liberation, they aspire.

Skyward Whispers

Gentle breezes, secrets tell,
Of loves and dreams that softly swell,
In skies where whispers freely roam,
In azure waves, their endless home.

Each cloud a letter, white and pure,
Messages in misty allure,
Hidden thoughts the skies convey,
In twilight's calm, in break of day.

Stars that twinkle, voices bright,
In the canvas of the night,
Echoes in the silent sweep,
Of cosmic wonders vast and deep.

Moonlight writes in silvered beams,
On night's soft veil, it gently gleams,
Stories of the hearts that soar,
Skyward whispers evermore.

Through the vault, the whispers glide,
On the wings of time, they ride,
In the silence, softly kissed,
By skyward whispers, love persists.

Nomadic Inspiration

Footsteps trace the sands of time,
In every path, a whispered rhyme,
Nomadic hearts, forever roam,
In endless quest, their boundless home.

Underneath the nomad's hat,
Dreams are spun, alive and fat,
Stories woven through the night,
In their journey, pure delight.

Wind and sky, their constant kin,
Where new tales and truths begin,
Every dawn, a canvas new,
Nomadic souls, the colors blue.

From desert dunes to forest green,
Every sight a vivid scene,
In paths unknown, the heart confides,
A flicker bright where hope resides.

Endless roadways, endless skies,
In every tear, a joy that lies,
Nomadic spirit, free and true,
Inspiration's light, with every view.

Fleeting Moments

In the whisper of the morning dew,
Time slips swiftly, like a breeze,
Memories sparkle, fresh and true,
Yet fade away with ease.

The sun climbs high, shadows shorten,
We grasp these relics, small and bright,
In the rush to savor golden,
Moments lost to time's swift flight.

As twilight lingers, a tender sigh,
We hold to visions, faint, refracted,
From dusk till dawn, the stars comply,
To life's brief dance, contracted.

Eternal Essence

In the heart's serene embrace,
Whispers of the eternal glow,
Light transcends both time and space,
Secrets only souls can know.

Nature's pulse, a constant beat,
Threads untouched by fleeting years,
Dreams and echoes softly meet,
Binding past through joyful tears.

We seek the essence, pure and true,
Beyond the veil of worldly strife,
In every breath, the ancient anew,
An endless dance, the song of life.

Beyond Chains

Beneath the weight, the burdened cry,
Hands and hearts in search of flight,
Rising wills that dare defy,
Shadows cast in pale light.

With every shackle, courage grows,
In the ember's quiet glow,
Hope within the spirit flows,
In freedom's wind, we rise and go.

Beyond the chains, the horizon calls,
A realm where dreams unchained reside,
In every tear, the barrier falls,
We journey forth, with strength as guide.

Unveiled Paths

Beneath the veil of foggy mist,
Paths revealed in sunlit gleam,
Guarded secrets, nature's tryst,
Guiding us through rivers' seam.

Each step forward, a whispered song,
Untold stories in the leaves,
In the quiet, we belong,
Find the truth that time conceives.

Unseen roads laid bare at last,
Journeys bold in twilight's cast,
Hearts unbound from shadows past,
Towards the light, our fate recast.

The Untamed Spirit

In the heart of untamed wild,
Roars the spirit, fierce and free,
Nature's truth, both rough and mild,
Echoes through the boundless sea.

An anthem to the unchained heart,
Whispering winds and roots so deep,
From dawn's first light, we never part,
In night's embrace, our secrets keep.

No cage can hold the soul's pure zest,
No chain can bind the yearning call,
In freedom's breath, we find our rest,
The untamed spirit, standing tall.

Horizons Unveiled

Beyond the edge, the sky does bend,
With hues of gold that never end.
Mountains whisper, oceans hum,
In nature's grasp, we're overcome.

A canvas painted, vast and wide,
With secrets veiled, in clouds they hide.
The sun dips low, yet hope remains,
In twilight's glow, we break our chains.

Chasing dreams in fields of light,
Through dawn's embrace, we'll take our flight.
To lands unknown, our hearts will sail,
New horizons to unveil.

Time stands still, in moments rare,
Where love and dreams fill open air.
In this dance of life's grand sweep,
We sow the seeds of what we'll reap.

Together, facing winds so wild,
Our spirits free, our hearts beguiled.
In unity, we find our way,
Through horizons, come what may.

Whispering Freedom

In quiet woods where shadows play,
With gentle breezes, we will sway.
The leaves that rustle, secrets keep,
In freedom's arms, our dreams will seep.

Through paths untrodden, whispers glide,
On wings of hope, our spirits ride.
The moon will guide, the stars will tell,
Of wanderers who broke their shell.

Freedom's voice, a tender call,
In every leaf and waterfall.
With open hearts, we heed the song,
To realms where we truly belong.

Mountains tall and rivers wide,
In the vast and wild, we find our stride.
For freedom's whisper sets us free,
To be the change we long to see.

In silent nights and breaking dawn,
New dreams are birthed where old are gone.
For every soul that dares to roam,
Freedom's whisper leads them home.

Boundaries Melt Away

Upon the vast, the borders fade,
In twilight's hues, a bond is made.
With every step, a line erased,
In heart's embrace, our fears are faced.

Once rigid walls of stone and steel,
Now melt away as hearts reveal.
Through open fields, and skies so wide,
We walk together, side by side.

No longer chained by fate's design,
We break the ties that once confined.
In unity, we cast away,
The chains that bound us, yesterday.

With courage bold, we pave the way,
Where love and hope in light convey.
For every boundary born of fear,
Dissolves when compassion draws near.

The world anew, in colors bright,
Is painted by our shared insight.
For when we stand as one, we say,
Watch all the boundaries melt away.

Flight of the Phoenix

From ashes cold, a spark is born,
A beacon in the breaking morn.
With wings of fire, it takes to sky,
A testament that we won't die.

Through trials vast and shadows deep,
The phoenix soars, no fear to keep.
Reborn from pain, it finds its grace,
In each new dawn, a shining face.

The scars of past, a badge of pride,
Through every storm, it learns to glide.
With flames that dance in evening's glow,
Eternal strength, from strife, will grow.

In every soul, the spark awaits,
A chance to rise from dire straits.
With courage found in darkest night,
We'll soar anew in phoenix flight.

From dusk to dawn, the cycle spins,
With each rebirth, a soul begins.
In endless flight, we find our might,
Through phoenix eyes, the world ignites.

Infinite Soul Songs

In the silence of the night,
Whispers of stars take flight.
Echoes of an endless tune,
Beneath the watchful moon.

Unseen, unheard, they roam,
In the vastness they call home.
Boundless symphonies they sing,
In gardens where dreams spring.

Each note a tale untold,
Melodies both new and old.
Infinite as the sky above,
Laden with timeless love.

Harmony in every breath,
From the cradle to the death.
Songs of joy, cries of mourn,
Since the day the world was born.

In the hearts they find a place,
In the soul's secret space.
Vows of eternal time,
The endless, ceaseless rhyme.

The Liberated Heart

Shackled dreams now unconfined,
By chains no longer bind.
Wings unfurl in the light,
Soaring to new heights.

Each beat a tale of grace,
In an infinite, open space.
A spirit free, unrestrained,
By love unfeigned.

Bonds of yesterday dissolve,
Frozen fears now evolve.
Journey to horizons far,
Guided by a star.

Rhythms of joy and peace,
An endless sweet release.
Heartbeats sync with song,
Of a world where souls belong.

Embrace the endless flight,
Guided by gentle light.
Liberated heart ever flies,
In the boundless skies.

Souls in the Open Sky

We are but whispers on the breeze,
Wandering through skies with ease.
Boundless spirits in flight,
In the day, in the night.

Stars as our eternal guide,
On this journey far and wide.
Converging in the twilight glow,
For secrets we yearn to know.

In the open realms of dreams,
Where nothing's as it seems.
We dance on twilight beams,
Bound by celestial themes.

Hearts unburdened by time,
In this cosmic rhyme.
United in a boundless span,
Eternity's grand plan.

We are the whispers of the song,
In the void, where souls belong.
Infinite and unconfined,
Through the skies, we find.

Flights of a Nomadic Heart

Untethered by lands or seas,
A heart that forever flees.
Chasing the horizon's light,
In the quiet of the night.

Nomadic dreams take flight,
Under the moon so bright.
A wanderer through space,
Finding heaven's embrace.

Destiny not drawn in sand,
Nor by the human hand.
In the winds, there's a song,
Where nomadic hearts belong.

Whispers of forgotten lore,
In places unexplored before.
Echoes in valleys deep,
Where ancient secrets sleep.

In every step, there's a call
To rise above the earthly sprawl.
Flights of the soul that start,
In the depths of a nomadic heart.

Beyond Silent Chains

Beyond silent chains where echoes rest,
In valleys deep, a heart's request,
To feel the freedom of the breeze,
And whisper secrets to the trees.

Where shadows part and dawn ascends,
The spirit wakes, the night unbends,
A journey starts with broken ties,
To seek a place where dreamers rise.

In fields of gold, the whispers cease,
The heart finds solace, deepened peace,
With every step, the chains dissolve,
A world anew, where spirits evolve.

No longer bound by darkened past,
We rise above, and break at last,
To skies where endless hope remains,
A life reborn beyond silent chains.

Sky without Anchors

A sky without anchors, a soul set free,
To ride the currents, wild and free,
No tethers hold the fates aloft,
Among the clouds so high and soft.

Horizons stretch beyond the eye,
Where dreams take wing and spirits fly,
In open skies where hearts explore,
No chains can bind them anymore.

Beneath the stars, the night reveals,
A universe that always heals,
With every dawn a new escape,
To worlds unknown, to endless shapes.

A sky without anchors, vast and wide,
With boundless realms where we confide,
The freedom found in open air,
Where courage soars without a care.

The Solitary Traveler

The solitary traveler walks alone,
On roads where shadows softly roam,
With every step, a story gleams,
In silent whispers, in quiet dreams.

Through forests dense and deserts wide,
Where secrets of the earth reside,
A wanderer with heart of flame,
Seeks solace in the unknown name.

Beneath the stars, a path unfolds,
As nights grow dark and air turns cold,
Yet onward goes the traveler bold,
In search of treasures, tales untold.

Though paths diverge and trails may wind,
The solitary seeks to find,
A world where mysteries intertwine,
And solitude reveals the sign.

Winds of Boundless Hope

In the winds of boundless hope we find,
The courage to leave doubts behind,
With every gust that breathes anew,
A lightened heart, a clearer view.

Through valleys deep and mountains high,
We chase the call of boundless sky,
In every breeze a promise kept,
Through storm and calm, where dreams are met.

As tempests rage and skies may dark,
The spirit keeps a fleeting spark,
A flame that guides through night's embrace,
In winds that lead to boundless grace.

Upon those winds, our hopes ascend,
To places where the soul can mend,
And in their whisper, hearts elope,
On winds of endless, boundless hope.

Limitless Pathways

Under the sky's vast, endless dome,
We walk paths known and those unknown,
Where every step a tale does weave,
And every turn a dream's reprieve.

Mountains high and valleys deep,
In secrets ancient, whispers seep,
Paths unfold in twisted maze,
With every dawn, in golden blaze.

Rivers flow in silver streams,
Crossing realms of distant dreams,
Stars align to light our stride,
Infinite ways where hopes abide.

Winds of change in whispers speak,
Guiding hearts both strong and meek,
In every way a hidden truth,
In every choice, eternal youth.

Boundless roads and endless hues,
Every path a different muse,
Step by step, horizons gleam,
In paths of life, we find our dream.

Uncharted Freedom

Unseen roads and skies untamed,
Where spirits soar, unbound, unnamed,
Freedom's call in wild embrace,
In open lands, we find our grace.

Waves crash on unmapped shores,
In endless flight, the eagle soars,
Horizons stretch in vast array,
Sunsets burn in bold display.

Echoes of the world unknown,
Where hearts are wild, souls are shown,
Uncharted paths, we dare to tread,
With every step, a story spread.

Trailblaze through the forests deep,
In every shadow, secrets keep,
Bound by none, our hearts ignite,
In boundless freedom, pure delight.

In every breath, a world to taste,
In every moment, none to waste,
Unfurl our wings, refuse the ground,
In freedom's realm, we're truly found.

The Unfettered Quest

Beyond the stars, our journey lies,
In endless depths, our spirits rise,
An endless quest, no chains to bind,
In search of truths, the heart will find.

Through desert sands and oceans wide,
On paths of dreams, we gently glide,
Unfurl the maps within our mind,
In realms unknown, the most to find.

Mountains call with ancient songs,
In every peak, where soul belongs,
Questing eyes on worlds anew,
In every step, horizons grew.

Mystic realms in twilight glow,
In endless night, through whispers flow,
Unfenced fields and open skies,
In questing hearts, the spirit flies.

A journey far, our souls' behest,
In boundless realms, we find our best,
Unfettered hearts, forever quest,
In every dawn, the endless rest.

Souls Without Cages

Unbound by walls, our spirits fly,
In endless seas and open sky,
Where hearts unfurled and dreams align,
In freedom's light, our souls enshrine.

Beyond the lock, beyond the key,
Where every heart is wild and free,
In whispered winds, our spirits chase,
In open fields, we find our place.

No cages hold our boundless dreams,
In flowing rivers, endless streams,
Through open doors, our futures pass,
In boundless seas, our sails amass.

Every night and every dawn,
In every loss, in every won,
Souls unshackled, pure and wild,
In freedom's realm, forever styled.

Raise the banners of the free,
In hearts of gold and eyes to see,
Souls without cages, boundless flight,
In endless day and starry night.

Unraveled Boundaries

In twilight's hush, the edges blur,
Where dreams and reality conspire.
Whispers weave where shadows stir,
Unraveled threads of ancient fire.

Beneath the moon's soft silver glow,
Fences fall, and hearts take flight.
The borders fade, the rivers flow,
Unveiling secrets of the night.

In this space where limits fade,
Our spirits dance, untamed, free.
Journey within, our choices made,
To lands where we can truly be.

Horizons wide, the world expands,
Unseen realms await our dare.
Boundaries shift like desert sands,
Potential gleams in every stare.

In confluence of ether's breath,
We find the truth that sets apart.
Life's essence, freed from time's cruel death,
Unraveled boundaries of the heart.

Murmurs of Freedom

Across the vast and windswept shore,
Where fields of green embrace the skies.
An echo hums of times before,
With murmurs where the spirit flies.

In gentle breeze, the whisper calls,
A song of courage, bold and rare.
The chains that bind begin to fall,
And souls ascend with newfound flair.

The river's tale, a flowing script,
Of journeys bold and stories told.
Freedom's seed in hearts is gripped,
It blooms despite the world's hold.

Through valleys deep and mountains wide,
We chase the dawn, find strength to rise.
In every step, with love as guide,
Our wings unfold, we claim the skies.

The murmur grows, a thunderous cheer,
With every voice a testament.
To freedom's call, so loud and clear,
A boundless, wild sacrament.

Pathways of Light

In dawn's embrace, the journey starts,
The golden threads of morning break.
Each step a pulse of hopeful hearts,
On pathways of light, we all partake.

The shadows flee, the day unfolds,
A canvas bright with dreams on flight.
We walk through realms of tales untold,
Guided by beams so pure, so bright.

In forest depths and fields of green,
The light bestows its gentle grace.
Through every twist, the unseen scene,
Illuminates each hidden space.

The stars above, a timeless chart,
Their luminescence guides our quest.
With courage, joy within the heart,
We navigate life's noble test.

At twilight's hour, when night descends,
The pathways gleam, a sacred rite.
In cycles vast, with love that mends,
We journey on through realms of light.

Elevated Existence

Above the clouds, where eagles soar,
In realms untouched by sorrow's bend.
An elevated world to explore,
Where souls in harmony ascend.

On peaks that kiss the azure sky,
We find a breath unbound by fear.
Horizons stretch beyond the eye,
Infinite spaces crisp and clear.

In twilight's depth, the stars align,
To spell a path of ethereal might.
With every heartbeat, spirits shine,
Elevated in the cosmic light.

Through whispered winds and mountain hymns,
Our essence flows, serene and pure.
A symphony of ancient whims,
A truth beyond what we endure.

In this divine, exalted plane,
We blend as one, yet stand unique.
Existence finds its higher gain,
In boundless love and strength we seek.

Unconfined Echoes

In caverns deep, the whispers rise,
A story told beneath the skies.
Each note a memory, each chant a sigh,
Unconfined echoes never die.

Through ages past, their voices blend,
In endless loops they find no end.
In heartbeats soft and ocean tides,
The echoes breathe where love abides.

A song of old, in shadows cast,
A melody from distant past.
With every breeze, their tunes renew,
Unconfined echoes, tried and true.

Silent whispers, subtle cries,
Lingering where the past resides.
They dance in moonlight, serenade the night,
Unconfined echoes in endless flight.

In every corner of spirit's field,
A hidden truth, by time revealed.
In whispers soft, the echoes call,
Unconfined, they embrace us all.

Freedom's Call

Beyond the chains, the eagle soars,
Through azure skies, it freely roars.
A distant peak, a boundless glide,
A testament to freedom's pride.

In fields of green, the meadows sing,
Of all the joy that freedom brings.
With every dawn, a hope anew,
The spirit's rise, the heart's true view.

Boundaries fall in freedom's wake,
Each step a choice, each path we take.
The open arms of liberty,
Hold tight the dream, the brave, the free.

In forest shadows, rivers bright,
The call of freedom, pure delight.
With wings unfurled, we face the breeze,
In moments gold, our souls find ease.

The night is long, but dawn will break,
With freedom's call, our hearts awake.
A journey endless, skies so vast,
In freedom's arms, we find our past.

Unrestricted Harmonies

In symphonies that break the mold,
A tale of life, both young and old.
In every note, a world is seen,
Where unrestricted harmonies convene.

Through chords that dance on breezes light,
Their melodies cast day from night.
Each echoed line, yet unforeseen,
In unrestricted harmonies, serene.

A cello's hum, a violin's cry,
Together form a boundless sky.
Their notes entwine in perfect grace,
Unrestricted harmonies embrace.

The music flows, no bars in sight,
With freedom found in pure delight.
In every breath, and every scene,
Unrestricted harmonies convene.

With open hearts and souls in tune,
Their rhythms dance beneath the moon.
In waves of sound, they intertwine,
Unrestricted, so divine.

Open Roads Ahead

Beyond the horizon, dreams unfold,
In lands where stories yet untold.
With each new step, a path we tread,
In open roads that lie ahead.

The sun may set, the stars may guide,
A journey shared, with friends beside.
Through valleys deep, and peaks so high,
The open roads lead to the sky.

In every turn, a lesson lies,
In every dawn, a new surprise.
With open hearts, we forge the trail,
On open roads where spirits sail.

From dawn to dusk, with eyes so wide,
We seek the truths that life can't hide.
The open roads, forever spread,
Invite us to where dreams are led.

With hope as fuel, and faith as light,
We journey forth into the night.
On open roads ahead we tread,
Where endless dreams and love are fed.

Open Skies, Open Hearts

Under the expanse of boundless blue,
Dreams take flight, horizons anew.
Hearts open wide, free to start,
We find our path, a living art.

Winds whisper tales of distant lands,
Carried on hope, a guiding hand.
Stars shine bright, our compass true,
In open skies, love's bloom renew.

Mountains stand tall, guardians bold,
Ancient stories silently told.
Rivers weave through time and space,
Embrace the journey, life's embrace.

Clouds drift by, serene and free,
Mirroring the joy in you and me.
Through open skies, our spirits soar,
In open hearts, we seek for more.

Each sunset paints a canvas vast,
Memories treasured, forever last.
In twilight's glow, we find our place,
Under open skies, in love's embrace.

Essence of Emancipation

Chains unshackled, freedom's call,
Break the barriers, rise from the fall.
Wings unbound, soar high and wide,
Embrace the light, let shadows hide.

Voices once muted now sing loud,
Breaking free from stifling shroud.
Hearts now dance in boundless glee,
Essence of emancipation, we decree.

Fear's grip loosening, courage found,
In unity, let freedom resound.
Through trials faced, we find our might,
Guided by truth, a beacon bright.

Rise up from the ashes of despair,
With strength renewed, conquer the air.
In every pulse, in every beat,
Freedom's essence, pure and sweet.

Dreams now flourish, unconfined,
A symphony of liberated minds.
In liberty's embrace we'll find,
The essence of emancipation, intertwined.

Beyond the Frame

Gaze beyond the gilded frame,
Where shadows dance and whisper name.
Colors blend in twilight's hue,
Stories told in shades anew.

Brushstrokes bold, a canvas wide,
Within each stroke, emotions bide.
Beyond the frame, life's art unveiled,
In every line, a tale regaled.

Eyes that see beyond the sight,
Find beauty hidden in the light.
In every crease, in every line,
A world of wonder, pure, divine.

Frames defined by mind's own art,
Boundary bent by open heart.
In every hue, in every shade,
A masterpiece of life portrayed.

Break the edges, journey still,
Beyond the frame, soul's spirit fill.
In every glance, a new story starts,
Beyond the frame, infinite hearts.

Unclasped Chains

Unclasped chains, the heart reborn,
Cast away the weight once worn.
In fields of freedom, we now tread,
Unfettered souls, by dreams we're led.

A future bright, no longer bound,
In open sky, our spirits found.
Voices rise in joyous refrain,
Echoed songs, end of the pain.

Crystal waters, clear and pure,
Reflect a world, of hope, for sure.
With every step in freedom's lands,
Our fate now rests in open hands.

Mountains high no longer staid,
Barriers broken, progress made.
In unity, we carve our way,
To brighter dawn, a brand-new day.

Chains now shattered on the ground,
Silent past, where we're not found.
With freedom's breath, our destiny reigns,
In hearts unbound, unclasped chains.

Embracing the Infinite

Under stars, where whispers blend,
Eternity begins, no end.
Hearts with cosmos, tend an ear,
To the infinite, crystal clear.

Time dissolves in night's embrace,
Galaxies, their paths to trace.
Questions fold in silence deep,
In the void, our secrets keep.

Infinite sky, a boundless hue,
Ancient dreams in silver hue.
Horizons stretch, forever wide,
In wonder, hand in hand, we glide.

Mysteries in shadows glow,
Reveal the truths we yearn to know.
Universe, a timeless scroll,
In its depths, we find our soul.

Stars align, our spirits free,
In the infinite, we cease to be.
Journey ends, where dreams ignite,
Embracing dark, yet full of light.

Unleashed Journeys

On paths unmarked, with hearts we tread,
Where wild winds whisper, fears are shed.
Life's adventure, free and grand,
Unleashed journeys, hand in hand.

Mountains call with voices clear,
Summits reached, we conquer fear.
Rivers flow through valleys wide,
In their currents, dreams abide.

Echoes of the past, now gone,
Footprints fade with each new dawn.
Horizons glowing, ever near,
Unleashing courage, conquering fear.

Voyages beneath the sky,
Untamed realms where spirits fly.
Each new step, a tale unfolds,
In our hearts, its truth we hold.

Boundless oceans, we explore,
Charting courses, seeking more.
Journeys end, where vistas gleam,
In the quest, we find our dream.

Bound for Nowhere

Paths uncharted, leading where,
In the mist, we find a dare.
Bound for nowhere, with the breeze,
Life's true meaning, yet to seize.

Wandering through fields untamed,
Questions posed, and answers claimed.
Echoes lost in twilight's glow,
In the void, our spirits flow.

Time's compass, lost in haze,
Shadows dance in fleeting gaze.
Unmapped trails, our feet embrace,
Bound for nowhere, find our place.

Whispers guide through night's expanse,
In the unknown, take a chance.
Every step, a path anew,
Bound for nowhere, skies of blue.

Dreams unfettered, free to roam,
In the vastness, find our home.
Journeys fade, yet ever clear,
In nowhere's heart, we persevere.

Skyward Wanderings

Eyes that chase the distant stars,
Through the night, beyond the bars.
Skyward hearts and minds take flight,
In the heavens, boundless light.

Clouds that whisper ancient tales,
Horizons where our dream prevails.
Winds that carry hopes anew,
Skyward wanderings, pure and true.

Galaxies in silken streams,
Guide our soul through endless dreams.
Moonlit paths that light our way,
Through the night to break of day.

Heavens vast, our spirits soar,
In their depths, we find our core.
Beyond the vast, yet close and near,
Skyward wanderings, skies so clear.

Among the stars, our hearts align,
In the dance of space and time.
Journey leads through endless night,
In skyward dreams, we find our light.

Winds of Wonder

Upon the hill, the breezes play,
A dance of light in skies of gray.
Leaves they whisper, tales are spun,
Of distant lands and setting sun.

Endless fields where grasses bend,
To the secrets that the winds commend.
Mountains echo whispered tunes,
Singing soft beneath the moons.

Children's laughter, soft and sweet,
Carried on the winds' retreat.
Through the valleys, through the trees,
It mingles with the murmuring seas.

In the evening, cool and clear,
Dreams take flight and far they steer.
Winds of wonder, wild and free,
Unfold their magic unto me.

Ancient stories, untold lore,
Guarded by the winds of yore.
In their current, I am found,
Boundless skies my soul surround.

Unchained Melodies

Notes that drift on evening air,
Melodies beyond compare.
Soft and subtle, bold and bright,
In the hush of twilight light.

Guided by a starry muse,
Harmonies of countless hues.
Each a thread of silken sound,
In a tapestry unbound.

Strings and voices, chimes and drums,
Gently where the moonlight hums.
Every heart a resonant string,
In the unchained melodies they sing.

Echoes of a distant call,
Fragments in the midnight hall.
Wandering thoughts and dreams take flight,
Carried through the endless night.

Eternal silence, broken free,
Lifts its veil in melody.
In the choir of the stars,
Melodies are our memoirs.

Emancipated Dreams

Dreams once tethered, now set free,
Soar across the endless sea.
Through the clouds and skies they climb,
To the edge of space and time.

Wings unbound, they grace the night,
Stars their lanterns, guiding light.
Hopes unleashed with fierce delight,
Turning darkness into bright.

No more chains and no more ties,
Lift their gaze to vast blue skies.
In the breeze of liberty,
Sing a song of victory.

Boundless like the ocean's waves,
Rise above what once enslaves.
Every whisper, every scream,
Echoes through the realm of dreams.

Freedom's horizon, endless span,
Marks the journey of each plan.
Emancipated, bold, and true,
Dreams arise in shades anew.

Brave New Horizons

Beyond the dawn, a world unknown,
In shadows cast by dreams we've sown.
Horizons beckon, bold and wide,
A call to brave the wild tide.

Mountains rise with snowy crest,
Oceans deep where secrets rest.
In these realms of the vast unseen,
Lies the heart of what we mean.

New horizons, bold and bright,
Carve a path through endless night.
Step by step, we claim our right,
In the journey toward the light.

Possibilities unfold,
Stories waiting to be told.
Each dawn's promise, fresh and new,
A canvas vast with endless hue.

Adventures call with voices clear,
To cast aside our doubt and fear.
Brave new horizons, here we stand,
With hope and courage, hand in hand.

Incessant Freedom

Upon the winds, my spirit flies,
Through endless realms, beneath the skies.
Unchained by time, unbound by fear,
The voice of freedom, ever-clear.

In silent whispers, freedom calls,
Beyond the earth, where sunlight falls.
With every breath, a new frontier,
The heart's embrace, forever near.

Through ancient lands and future years,
An endless journey, free from tears.
In boundless fields where dreams reside,
My soul, unbridled, seeks the tide.

The chains of earth, they fall away,
As twilight yields to break of day.
In realms of light, my spirit's song,
A testament to freedom strong.

Incessant freedom, pure and bright,
Guides me through the endless night.
With wings of faith, on winds I soar,
Bound by chains, no nevermore.

Self-Sown Wings

From seeds of hope, my wings have grown,
In fertile dreams, they've gently sown.
Against the dawn, my spirit sings,
To new horizons, self-sown wings.

In twilight's glow, they whisper low,
Of places where the wild things go.
With every beat, another chance,
To join the stars in cosmic dance.

Through forest deep and mountain high,
A bird of hope now learns to fly.
With feathers strong, and heart of light,
I take my leave, into the night.

With every gust, my doubts erase,
In boundless sky, I find my place.
No longer bound to earthly things,
I glide on dreams, with self-sown wings.

To heights unknown, my path is clear,
Unfettered by the weight of fear.
With open heart, the freedom brings,
The endless flight on self-sown wings.

Rhythms of Emancipation

In rhythms pulsed from cosmic drums,
The beat of freedom softly hums.
With every note, a chain undone,
The symphony of Time begun.

As dawn emerges, shadows fade,
In light of day, new paths are made.
Through melodies, the spirit's keen,
To dance where moons of freedom lean.

Beneath the stars, in open fields,
The whispers of emancipation yield.
With skies wide open, dreams take flight,
On wings of rhythm, pure and bright.

The heart, unbound, begins to soar,
In endless rhythms, evermore.
In every song, a history laced,
The freedom's dance, in time embraced.

In this harmonic, truths align,
In every beat, the spirit shines.
Rhythms of emancipation call,
To hearts set free, we rise, we fall.

Boundless Love Notes

On paper wings, my love takes flight,
Through realms of day, and dreams of night.
In every line, a story told,
Of hearts unbound, in love's pure gold.

In starlit skies, my whispers trace,
A boundless love in endless space.
Through silent echoes, voices blend,
In timeless notes, my heart I'll send.

A symphony of breath and time,
In every verse, our souls align.
With open arms and tender grace,
Our love's embrace, a sacred place.

With ink of stars and quill of dreams,
I pen the heart in moonlit beams.
No boundary binds, no border keeps,
The love that's written, love that leaps.

Eternal notes on breezes flow,
To places where the wildflowers grow.
In boundless realms, with hearts remote,
We live within these love-laced notes.

Whisper of a Roaming Heart

Through hills and dales it wanders free,
With gentle touch of winds' decree;
Where rivers twist, and mountains part,
It follows whispers, a roaming heart.

Beneath the moon's enchanting glow,
It treads where flowers shyly grow;
Each step a dance, each pause a sigh,
In search of dreams that never die.

In twilight's hush, the heart confides,
To nature's breath, it closely ties;
A journey inked by love and pain,
To feel, to lose, to find again.

The boundaries fade, no walls in sight,
It stretches out to touch the light;
A wanderer in night's embrace,
In stars it sees a fleeting trace.

Forever travels, never still,
The heart that roams by sheer will;
Wherever whispers gently start,
There journeys on, the roaming heart.

Embrace the Open Vast

Upon the cliffs where seagulls soar,
The open vast invites implore;
Embrace the winds, the waves that crash,
A symphony both wild and brash.

Sand beneath the traveler's feet,
An endless blue with sounds so sweet;
Horizons call with whispers soft,
A beckoning both near and oft.

Courage finds in vastness grand,
The heart to leave, the will to stand;
To chase the whispers, bold and free,
In open arms of endless sea.

Mountains high and valleys wide,
A path unfolds, no need to hide;
Each step a vow to taste and see,
What lies beyond, embraced in spree.

With open heart and open eyes,
Beneath the ever-changing skies;
A soul set free to wander past,
Into the wondrous, open vast.

Freefall into the Stars

In twilights deep, where silence glows,
A cosmic dance begins, it flows;
With constellations graced in light,
We freefall into endless night.

Nebulas like whispers swirl,
Midnight's canvas starts to twirl;
Guided by the realms afar,
We find our way among the stars.

Each moment passed in velvet skies,
A journey framed by starlit eyes;
The universe, a boundless chart,
Where dreams and wishes freely start.

Galaxies of hopes untold,
In stardust trails our hands we hold;
The unknown vast in silent song,
To this astral place we do belong.

We let go, released from fears,
To realms where light outshines the years;
In cosmic dance's loving arms,
We freefall deep into the stars.

Echoes of Emancipation

Beneath the chains of yesterday,
Lie echoes of a brighter way;
Within the heart, a cry set free,
To voice the tunes of liberty.

In shadows cast by bygone fears,
A whisper grows through silent years;
A note of hope, a song reborn,
From darkness breaks a sunlit morn.

With every step, the shackles fall,
A dance of freedom, triumph's call;
The spirits rise on winds of change,
In harmony, their voices range.

Echoes bounce off mountain peaks,
Resound through valleys, rivers, creeks;
A symphony of souls unbound,
In freedom's light they all are found.

Forever rings this liberating sound,
Beyond the earth, the sky, the ground;
A testament to spirits bold,
In echoes free, their stories told.

Detached Footprints

On sandy shores, their whispers fade
Where waves erase the paths we've made
Silent stories in grains of white
Fade with each kiss of morning light

A trail of dreams on twilight's edge
Soft imprints mark the water's pledge
Each step a past, a tale untold
Lost in the tide's embrace, so cold

Memories cast in silhouettes
Footprints linger, soft regrets
As seabirds chase the setting sun
In fleeting moments, we are one

The moonlight paints a silver line
Shared steps dissolve in brine
Yet echoes of our wanderings stay
In timeless dance of night and day

And when the sea reclaims the shore
Our steps are bound no more
Detached from earth, they float away
To unseen realms where spirits play

Freefall into Freedom

From towering heights, the leap we take
Into the vast and boundless skies
No chains to bind, no ropes to break
Just endless blue and echoing cries

With arms spread wide and hearts unchained
We soar through space, through clouds, through dreams
The shackles of earth so faint, so waned
In freedom's pure and radiant beams

The wind, a whisper in our ears
Tells tales of lands we've yet to see
In every rush, in every cheer
We taste the thrill of being free

The ground grows distant, far below
A memory of lives gone by
In this great dive, we come to know
The boundless spirit's sweetest high

And when we land, where'er it be
Our souls remember what they found
In freefall's grace, in sky's decree
A freedom pure, without a bound

Drifting in Light

In morning's gleam, where shadows melt
A world bathed in a golden hue
We find a peace we've never felt
In rays that pierce the skies so blue

Drifting softly, in light's embrace
We float on dreams that sunlight weaves
A gentle touch, a warm caress
In this soft glow, our hearts believe

The world beneath us fades away
In mists and sparkles, soft and bright
We wander through the break of day
In paths of luminescent light

Each ray a guide, a whispered song
Leading us through cosmic tides
In luminance where we belong
We let the shining currents guide

In light, we drift, pure and serene
No shadows cast, no darkness known
A voyage through a radiant dream
Where light and soul are deeply sewn

Infinite Meanderings

Along the stream of endless flows
We wander, seeking hidden truths
In currents where eternity grows
And time wears ever-youthful hues

Infinite paths, in winding dance
Through forests dense, through valleys wide
Each twist and turn, a second chance
To find ourselves in nature's stride

Lost in the shift of sun and shade
We drift through realms both near and far
Where earth and sky and dreams are made
And wonders spark like distant stars

With every step, a story spins
An epic woven, step by step
In meanderings where life begins
And endless journeys intercept

In ceaseless wander, hearts unwind
Through lands unknown, by rivers grand
In infinite meanders, we find
A boundless world at our command

The Unpaved Road

Through forests dense and shadows long,
Whispered winds sing nature's song.
Pebbles crunch beneath worn feet,
On paths where earth and sky do meet.

Unseen hands do nudge and guide
Travelers on this rugged ride.
Roots entwined form upward stairs,
Leading hearts past worldly cares.

Each footprint tells a tale of old,
Of wanderers both young and bold.
In twilight's glow, the road reveals
Dreams once hidden now unsealed.

Boundless Odysseys

Sail across the star-strewn skies,
Where the moon's reflection lies.
Galaxies in endless dance,
Inviting souls to take a chance.

Voyages through time and space,
Charted by hearts on an endless chase.
Constellations form the maps,
Guiding dreamers from their traps.

Winds of change both fierce and kind,
Push the sails of the curious mind.
Horizons stretch beyond the mist,
A world by stars and sunlit kissed.

Freefall into Wholeness

In the void where silence dwells,
Traces of the sacred swell.
A leap of faith, a boundless dive,
Where fragmented souls revive.

Gravity's gentle tender touch,
Cradling hearts that seek so much.
Through the blur of space and air,
Inner peace becomes the fare.

Let the wind unveil the truth,
Reclaim the innocence of youth.
In unity, the self concealed,
Finds the wholeness once concealed.

Disentangled Breath

Inhale the sun's eternal light,
Exhale shadows, take to flight.
Breath untangles webs of fear,
Setting minds so crystal clear.

With each breath, the spirit glows,
Shedding weight from ancient woes.
Calm descends on hearts distressed,
In rhythm, bodies come to rest.

Every pulse a soothing wave,
Washing free a soul once grave.
Inner balance softly weaves,
A tapestry of life received.

9 789916 860724